THE MARRIAGE QUOTATION BOOK

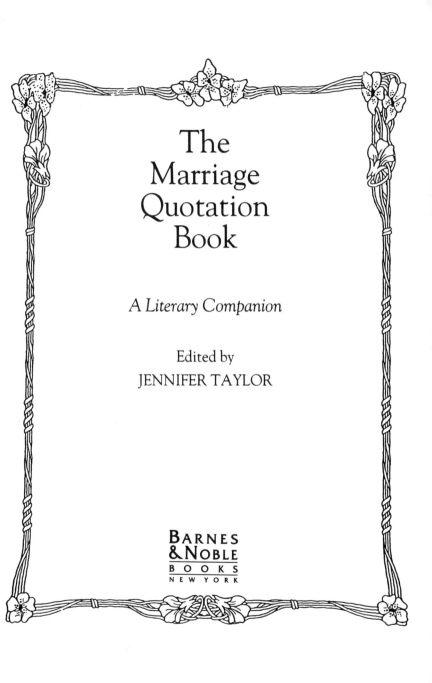

The Marriage Quotation Book

A Literary Companion

Edited by
JENNIFER TAYLOR

BARNES
&NOBLE
BOOKS
NEW YORK

This edition published by Marboro Books Corp.,
a division of Barnes & Noble, Inc.,
by arrangement with Robert Hale, Ltd.

1992 Barnes & Noble Books

ISBN 0-88029-883-9

Printed and bound in the United States of America

M 9 8 7 6 5 4 3 2 1

Preface

 The subject of marriage has brought out the wit – and often the vitriol – of writers down the centuries, and certainly, as one reads through aphorisms, plays and novels, the balance seems to be against it. D.H. Lawrence was one who believed that marriage as an institution would not last, and that the 'hated yoke of conjugality' would be abolished as soon as a social substitute could be found for it.

And yet, as is pointed out often enough, marriage remains remarkably popular despite the high divorce statistics, and although there has never been less incentive for it in the first place.

Unsurprisingly the majority of critical quotes comes from men who have found 'the yoke' irksome, and the same images keep on cropping up through literature – the marital knot and the noose, shackles and fetters. 'Wife' was found at a very early date to rhyme with 'strife', and cockney rhyming slang for 'wife' over the last two hundred years has included 'bit of tripe', 'carving-knife', 'drum and fife' and 'trouble and strife', while 'joy of my life' has invariably been used in a jocular context. Jokes and circumlocutions abound: in modern times, Rumpole's 'She Who Must Be Obeyed' in John Mortimer's series, and

Arthur's *wary approach to 'Her Indoors' in the television series* Minder *spring to mind. The language does not seem to be as rich in expressions for husbands, although jokes about hen-pecked husbands wearing the petticoats and about cuckolds are centuries old. Men have certainly not had it all their own way.*

Lady novelists whose province is the human heart and its ties, from Jane Austen to Susan Ferrier and Edith Wharton, have on the whole written with fairness and balance of the rights and obligations of relationships. Meanwhile women of less literary bent have traditionally found their outlet in the form of nagging. As Douglas Jerrold observed of his Mrs Caudle, 'she was not a woman to wear chains without shaking them'. Could Eve herself have been guilty now and then of a lecture? The strident Mrs Caudle's persistent nagging evidently struck a few chords since the book, Mrs Caudle's Curtain Lectures, *was translated into a number of European languages within a few years of its publication in 1846; amusingly, the Italian edition was subtitled* 'Esercizi di conversazione per gli studenti della inglese' – *conversation exercises for students of English.*

This short selection from the rich pickings offered by literature attempts to cover a range of attitudes and situations, and problems. The many 'wictims o' connubiality' – to use Sam Weller's words in The Pickwick Papers – *are more often than not the victims of unrealistic expectations as young lovers who think they are embarking on eternal ecstasy come face to face with prosaic reality. Sadly there are not many Darby and Joans in literature, probably because a happy marriage doesn't make 'good copy': there is little more to say than 'And they lived happily ever after', as in the best fairy-tales. But for an expression of lasting married love one can do no better than the letters exchanged between Elizabeth Hervey and her husband the Earl of Bristol in the early eighteenth century.*

Preface

Edith Wharton, in her novel The Age of Innocence, called a wedding 'a rite that seemed to belong to the dawn of history'. Marriage, as Tertullian observed, seems likely to carry on until the end of time.

JENNIFER TAYLOR

The marriage state, with or without the affection suitable to it, is the completest image of Heaven and Hell we are capable of receiving in this life.
RICHARD STEELE
The Spectator

For what is wedlock forced but a hell,
An age of discord and continual strife?
Whereas the contrary bringeth bliss,
And is a pattern of celestial peace.
SHAKESPEARE
Henry VI, Part 1

Well-married, a man is winged: ill-matched, he is shackled.
HENRY WARD BEECHER
Proverbs from Plymouth Pulpit

Marriage is neither heaven nor hell, it is simply purgatory.
ABRAHAM LINCOLN

Mariages (as they say) are made in heauen, though consumated in yearth.
> JOHN LYLY
> *Euphues and his England*, 1580

What is there in the vale of life
Half so delightful as a wife,
When friendship, love, and peace combine
To stamp the marriage bond divine?
> WILLIAM COWPER
> 'Love Abused'

Whoso findeth a wife findeth a good thing, and obtaineth favour of the Lord.
> PROVERBS, 18:22

Marriage is not a good, but it is a good in comparison with fornication.
> ST AUGUSTINE
> *On the Good of Marriage*

On what pretence can man have interdicted marriage, which is a law of nature? It is as though we were forbidden to eat, to drink, to sleep.
> MARTIN LUTHER
> *Table-Talk*

Marriage itself among all races is for the one purpose of procreating children ...; marriage was instituted for this purpose, so that children might be born properly and decently.
> ST AUGUSTINE
> *On the Good of Marriage*

No man is so virtuous as to marry a wife only to have children.
>   MARTIN LUTHER
>   *Table-Talk*

To the contract of marriage, besides the man and wife, there is a third party – Society; and, if it be considered as a vow – GOD: and, therefore, it cannot be dissolved by their consent alone.
>   SAMUEL JOHNSON
>   Boswell's *Life of Johnson*

The Church, celibate as its priesthood may be, ... really rests upon the indissolubility of marriage. Make marriage in any serious degree unstable, dissoluble, destroy the permanency of marriage, and the Church falls.
>   D.H. LAWRENCE
>   *A Propos of Lady Chatterley's Lover*

Marriage lies at the bottom of all government.
>   CONFUCIUS
>   *The Book of Rites*

The only secure basis for a present day State is the welding of its units in marriage, but there is rottenness and danger at the foundations of the State if many of the marriages are unhappy. To-day, particularly in the middle classes in this country, marriage is far less really happy than its surface appears.
>   MARIE STOPES
>   *Married Love*, 1918

Marriage has, as you say, no *natural* relation to love. Marriage belongs to society; it is a social contract.
SAMUEL TAYLOR COLERIDGE
Table-Talk

I believe marriages would in general be as happy, and often more so, if they were all made by the Lord Chancellor, upon a due consideration of characters and circumstances, without the parties having any choice in the matter.
SAMUEL JOHNSON
Boswell's *Life of Johnson*

As to marriage or celibacy, let a man take which course he will, he will be sure to repent.
SOCRATES

Marriage is a mistake of youth – which we should all make.
DON HEROLD
American humorist

One was never married, and that's his hell; another is, and that's his plague.
ROBERT BURTON
Anatomy of Melancholy

Wen you're a married man, Samivel, you'll understand a good many things as you don't understand now; but vether it's worth while goin' through so much to learn so little, as the charity boy said ven he got to the end of the alphabet, is a matter o' taste.
CHARLES DICKENS
The Pickwick Papers

Marriage is like a cage; the birds outside are desperate to get in, and those inside equally desperate to get out.

> MONTAIGNE
> *Essais*

Unlived life is a destructive and irresistible force working quietly but relentlessly. The result is that the married woman begins to doubt marriage. The unmarried woman believes in it, because she desires marriage.

> C.G. JUNG
> *Psychological Reflections*

Marriage is a lottery in which men stake their liberty and women their happiness.

> VIRGINIE DES RIEUX
> *Epigrams*

But married once, a man is stak'd or pown'd, and cannot graze beyond his own hedge.

> PHILIP MASSINGER
> *Fatal Dowry*, 1632

A married man turns his staff into a stake.

> ENGLISH PROVERB

Husbands are like lots in the lottery: you may draw forty blanks before you find one that has any prize in him.

> JOHN MARSTON
> *The Dutch Courtesan*, 1605

Marriage is a lottery, but you can't tear up your ticket if you lose.

> F.M. KNOWLES
> *A Cheerful Year Book*

Wedlock's a lane where there is no turning.
> DINAH M.M. CRAIK
> *Magnus and Morna*

Wedlock is a padlock.
> JOHN RAY
> *English Proverbs*

Holy Deadlock.
> A.P. HERBERT
> title of novel

Marry'd in haste, we oft repent at leisure;
Some by experience find these words misplaced,
Marry'd at leisure, they repent in haste.
> BENJAMIN FRANKLIN
> *Poor Richard*

Some men ... saye it goeth by destenye To hange or wed ...
I am well sure Hangynge is better of the twayne Sooner
done, and shorter payne.
> W. HORMAN
> *The Schoolhouse of Women*, 1541

Suspicion, Discontent, and Strife,
Come in for Dowry with a wife.
> ROBERT HERRICK
> 'His Comfort'

Marriage is like life in this – that it is a field of battle, and
not a bed of roses.
> ROBERT LOUIS STEVENSON
> *Virginibus Puerisque*

Though women are angels, yet wedlock's the devil.
> BYRON
> *Hours of Idleness*

If I were married to a hogshead of claret, matrimony would make me hate it.
> JOHN VANBRUGH
> *The Provok'd Wife*

Marriage halves our griefs, doubles our joys, and quadruples our expenses.
> ENGLISH PROVERB

Every man plays the fool once in his life, but to marry is playing the fool all one's life long.
> WILLIAM CONGREVE

The bachelor is a peacock, the engaged man a lion, and the married man a jackass.
> GERMAN PROVERB

Get thee to a nunnery, go; farewell. Or, if thou wilt needs marry, marry a fool; for wise men know well enough what monsters you make of them.
> SHAKESPEARE
> *Hamlet*

There's one fool at least in every married couple.
> HENRY FIELDING
> *Amelia*

Too long has marriage, in this tasteless age,
With ill-bred raillery supply'd the stage;
No little scribbler is of wit so bare,
But has his fling at the poor wedded pair.
　　JOSEPH ADDISON
　　The Drummer

As there is nothing in the world as common as marriage,
and as it is something over which men commonly make
fools of themselves, it is hardly surprising that it should
form the subject matter of most comedies.
　　MOLIÈRE
　　preface to *Le Mariage forcé*

Marriage ... notwithstanding all the loose talk of the
Town, the Satires of antient, or modern Pretenders to Wit,
will never lose its just Esteem from the Wise and Good.
　　MARY ASTELL
　　Reflections Upon Marriage, 1700

Venus, a beautiful good-natured lady, was the goddess of
love; Juno, a terrible shrew, the goddess of marriage; and
they were always mortal enemies.
　　JONATHAN SWIFT

'Tis melancholy, and a fearful sign
Of human frailty, folly, also crime,
That love and marriage rarely can combine,
Although they both are born in the same clime.
　　BYRON
　　Don Juan

18

How oft, when press'd to marriage, have I said,
Curse on all laws but those which Love has made!
Love, free as air, at sight of human ties,
Spreads his light wings, and in a moment flies.
ALEXANDER POPE
'Eloisa to Abelard'

Question: 'Is it possible for true love to exist in marriage?'

Judgment of the Countess of Champagne: 'Our ruling is hereby that love cannot extend its dominion over a married couple. For lovers indeed grant each other everything in all freedom, without the constraint of any obligation, whereas husband and wife are bound by duty not to refuse each other anything.

Delivered in the year 1174, the third day of the calends of May.
medieval code of love drawn up by 'Andreas the chaplain', quoted by STENDHAL in *De L'Amour*

The Lion is the King of Beasts, but he is scarcely suitable for a domestic pet. In the same way, I suspect love is rather too violent a passion to make a good domestic sentiment.
ROBERT LOUIS STEVENSON
Virginibus Puerisque

There can be only one end to marriage without love, and that is love without marriage.
JOHN CHURTON COLLINS
Victorian literary critic

I don't think matrimony consistent with the liberty of the subject.
GEORGE FARQUHAR

Sir, it is so far from being natural for a man and woman to live in a state of marriage, that we find all the motives which they have for remaining in that connection, and the restraints which civilized society imposes to prevent separation, are hardly sufficient to keep them together.

> SAMUEL JOHNSON
> Boswell's *Life of Johnson*

There was already at that time debate about the rights of women, and about the relations between married couples, their rights and freedom ... But Natasha took no interest in such issues, and did not even understand them. Then, as now, those questions existed only for people who see nothing in marriage beyond the pleasure which husband and wife may derive from one another, and fail to see its whole significance which lies in the family.

> LEO TOLSTOY
> *War and Peace*

Man and wife, a king and queen with one or two subjects, and a few square yards of territory of their own: this, really, is marriage. It is true freedom because it is a true fulfilment, for man, woman, and children.

> D.H. LAWRENCE
> *A Propos of Lady Chatterley's Lover*

'One does have the feeling that marriage is a *pis aller*,' he admitted.

'Then don't do it,' said Birkin, 'I tell you,' he went on, 'the same as I've said before, marriage in the old sense seems to me repulsive. *Egoïsme à deux* is nothing to it. It's a sort of tacit hunting in couples: the world all in couples, each couple in its own little house, watching its own little interests, and stewing in its own little privacy – it's the most repulsive thing on earth.'

    D.H. LAWRENCE
    Women in Love

We are just in the throes of a great revolt against marriage, a passionate revolt against its ties and restrictions. In fact, at least three-quarters of the unhappiness of modern life could be laid at the door of marriage ... And everybody, pretty well, takes it for granted that as soon as we can find a possible way out of it, marriage will be abolished.

    D.H. LAWRENCE
    A Propos of Lady Chatterley's Lover

And when will there be an end of marrying? I suppose, when there is an end of living!

    TERTULLIAN
    An Exhortation to Chastity

I think a man and a woman should choose each other for life, for the simple reason that a long life with all its accidents is barely enough for a man and a woman to understand each other; and in this case to understand is to love.

    JOHN BUTLER YEATS
    Letters to His Son

Wives are young men's mistresses, companions for middle age, and old men's nurses.

    FRANCIS BACON
    Essays

What marriage may be in the case of two persons of cultivated faculties, identical in opinions and purposes, between whom there exists that best kind of equality, similarity of powers and capacities with reciprocal superiority in them, so that each can enjoy the luxury of looking up to the other ... I will not attempt to describe.

> JOHN STUART MILL
> *The Subjection of Women*, 1869

In most good marriages, the woman is her husband's closest friend and adviser.

> NANCY REAGAN
> quoted in *The Sunday Times*, December 1989

I'll suffer no daughter of mine to play the fool with her heart, indeed! She shall marry for the purpose for which matrimony was ordained amongst people of birth – that is, for the aggrandisement of her family, the extending of their political influence – for becoming, in short, the depository of their mutual interest. These are the only purposes for which persons of rank ever think of marriage.

> SUSAN FERRIER
> *Marriage*, 1818

She herself had sought dignity and she thinks that everyone should follow her example. The boys will marry eventually but their brides must be carefully chosen; they will have to be of a suitable pattern to conform with the family destiny.

> ANITA BROOKNER
> *Family and Friends*

When he noticed that Charles blushed whenever he was near Emma, a sure sign that one of these days he would ask for her hand in marriage, père Rouault pondered the matter. Charles was rather a puny fellow, he thought, and was far from being an ideal son-in-law; but people said he was steady, and thrifty in his habits; he was well educated, and was unlikely to haggle too much over the dowry. And, as père Rouault was going to have to sell over forty acres of property shortly, and owed a lot of money to the builder ..., he made his mind up: Charles could have Emma if he asked for her.

> GUSTAVE FLAUBERT
> *Madame Bovary*

His designs were strictly honourable, as the saying is; that is, to rob a lady of her fortune by way of marriage.

> HENRY FIELDING
> *Tom Jones*

Remember, it is as easy to marry a rich woman as a poor woman.

> W.M. THACKERAY
> *Pendennis*

The woes of wedlock with the joys, we mix;
'Tis best repenting in a coach and six.

> SAMUEL GARTH
> *Cato*

My Lord Denbigh is going to marry a fortune, I forget her name; my Lord Gower asked him how long the honeymoon would last? He replied, 'Don't tell me of the honeymoon; it is harvest moon with me.'

    HORACE WALPOLE
    in a letter to George Montagu, 19 May 1756

The barbarous custom of wresting from women whatever she possesses, whether by inheritance, donation or her own industry, and conferring it all upon the man she marries, to be used at his discretion and will, perhaps waste it on his wicked indulgences, ... is such a monstrous perversion of *justice* by *law*, that we might well marvel how it could obtain in a Christian community.

    SARAH JOSEPHA HALE
    'The Rights of Married Women', *Godey's Lady's Book*, 1837

'... marrying merely to be married, to manage her own affairs, and have her own way – so childish! – or marrying merely to get an establishment – so base! How women, and such young creatures, *can* bring themselves to make these venal matches ...'

    MARIA EDGEWORTH
    Ormond, 1817

The sum and substance of female education in America, as in England, is training women to consider marriage as the sole object in life, and to pretend that they do not think so.

    HARRIET MARTINEAU
    'Women', *Society in America*, 1837

St Catherine, St Catherine, O lend me thine aid,
And grant that I never may die an old maid.
A husband, St Catherine,
A *good* one, St Catherine;
But arn-a-one better than
Narn-a-one, St Catherine.
Sweet St Catherine,
A husband, St Catherine,
Handsome, St Catherine,
Rich, St Catherine.

    ANON
    prayer to St Catherine, patron saint of spinsters

The women who take husbands not out of love but out of greed ... are whores in everything but name. The only difference between them and my girls is that my girls gave a man his money's worth.

    POLLY ADLER
    American madam, in *A House Is Not a Home*, 1953

Married women are kept women and they are beginning to find it out.

    LOGAN PEARSALL SMITH
    Afterthoughts

Marriage is a career which brings about more benefits than many others.

    SIMONE DE BEAUVOIR
    Le Deuxième Sexe

He reviewed his friends' marriages – the supposedly happy ones – and saw none that answered, even remotely, to the passionate and tender comradeship which he pictured as his permanent relation with May Welland. He perceived that such a picture presupposed, on her part, the experience, the versatility, the freedom of judgment, which she had been carefully trained not to possess; and with a shiver of foreboding he saw his marriage becoming what most of the other marriages about him were: a dull association of material and social interests held together by ignorance on the one side and hypocrisy on the other.

 EDITH WHARTON
 The Age of Innocence

A real marriage bears no resemblance to these marriages of interest or ambition. It is two lovers who live together. A priest may well say certain words, a notary may well sign certain papers – I regard these preparations in the same way that a lover regards the rope ladder that he ties to his mistress's window.

 LADY MARY WORTLEY MONTAGU
 Essay

Marriage, which has been the bourne of so many narratives, is still a great beginning, as it was to Adam and Eve, who kept their honeymoon in Eden, but had their first little one among the thorns and thistles of the wilderness. It is still the beginning of the home epic – the gradual conquest or irremediable loss of that complete union which makes the advancing years a climax, and age the harvest of sweet memories in common.

 GEORGE ELIOT
 Middlemarch

Love, the quest; marriage, the conquest; divorce, the inquest.

> HELEN ROWLAND
> American columnist

There are but two objects in marriage, love or money. If you marry for love, you will certainly have some very happy days, and probably many very uneasy ones; if for money, you will have no happy days and probably no uneasy ones.

> LORD CHESTERFIELD
> *Letters to His Son*

Who marries for love without money, has good nights and sorry days.

> ENGLISH PROVERB

Never marry but for love; but see that thou lovest what is lovely.

> WILLIAM PENN
> *Some Fruits of Solitude*, 1693

I want (who does not want?) a wife,
Affectionate and fair,
To solace all the woes of life,
And all its joys to share;
Of temper sweet, of yielding will,
Of firm yet placid mind,
With all my faults to love me still,
With sentiment refin'd.

> JOHN QUINCY ADAMS
> *Man Wants But Little*

'No,' thought she, 'it is not in splendour and distinction that I shall find happiness; it is in the cultivation of the domestic virtues – the peaceful joys of a happy home, and a loved companion, that my felicity must consist. Without these, I feel that I should still be poor, were I mistress of millions ... I shall never marry a man with twenty thousand a year, whom I would not have with five hundred.'

    SUSAN FERRIER
    Marriage, 1818

'I am not romantic you know. I never was. I ask only a comfortable home; and considering Mr Collins's character, connections, and situation in life, I am convinced that my chance of happiness with him is as fair, as most people can boast on entering the marriage state.'

    JANE AUSTEN
    Pride and Prejudice

Marriage, Sir, is much more necessary to a man than to a woman; for he is much less able to supply himself with domestick comforts. You will recollect my saying to some ladies the other day, that I had often wondered why young women should marry, as they have so much more freedom, and so much more attention paid to them while unmarried, than when married.

    SAMUEL JOHNSON
    Boswell's *Life of Johnson*

When a girl marries she exchanges the attentions of many men for the inattention of one.

    HELEN ROWLAND
    American columnist

When a man of thirty-five is happily, blissfully married, the scope of his reflections is necessarily limited ... He is no longer haunted by the face of every pretty girl he meets, for he has already met the woman most fitted in the wide world to make him happy ... He is no longer prone to dreams about the object of his affections, for he has her perpetually beside him.

> ROBERT GRANT
> *Reflections of a Married Man*, 1892

It had now entered Dorothea's mind that Mr Casaubon might wish to make her his wife, and the idea that he would do so touched her with a sort of reverential gratitude. How good of him – nay, it would be almost as if a winged messenger had suddenly stood beside her path and held out his hand towards her!

> GEORGE ELIOT
> *Middlemarch*

That is partly why women marry – to keep up the fiction of being in the hub of things.

> ELIZABETH BOWEN
> *The House in Paris*

Marriage is a lot of things ... but it is definitely not a partnership because that implies equal gain. And every right-thinking woman knows the profit in matrimony is by all odds hers.

> PHYLLIS McGINLEY
> *The Province of the Heart*, 1959

But Thérèse had possibly given in to a more deep-seated feeling ..., seeking in marriage ... a refuge. Was it not a feeling of panic which had made her rush into it? She had been a practical and domestically minded little girl, and she was in a hurry to find her pigeon-hole in life.

> FRANÇOIS MAURIAC
> *Thérèse Desqueyroux*

He was ready to be doomed. Marriage was like a doom to him. He was willing to condemn himself in marriage, to become like a convict condemned to the mines of the underworld, living no life in the sun, but having a dreadful subterranean activity. He was willing to accept this. And marriage was the seal of his condemnation.

> D.H. LAWRENCE
> *Women in Love*

'There is not one in a hundred of either sex who is not taken in when they marry. Look where I will, I see that it *is* so; and I feel that it *must* be so, when I consider that it is, of all transactions, the one in which people expect most from others, and are least honest themselves.'

> JANE AUSTEN
> *Mansfield Park*

Man scans with scrupulous care the character and pedigree of his horses, cattle, and dogs before he matches them; but when he comes to his own marriage he rarely, or never, takes any such care.

> CHARLES DARWIN
> *The Descent of Man*

If I married him,
I should not dare to call my soul my own
Which so he had bought and paid for ...
> ELIZABETH BARRETT BROWNING
> *Aurora Leigh*

'Well,' said Charlotte, 'I wish Jane success with all my heart; and if she were married to him to-morrow, I should think she had as good a chance of happiness, as if she were to be studying his character for a twelve-month. Happiness in marriage is entirely a matter of chance. If the dispositions of the parties are ever so well known to each other, or ever so similar before-hand, it does not advance their felicity in the least. They always continue to grow sufficiently unlike afterwards to have their share of vexation; and it is better to know as little as possible of the defects of the person with whom you are to pass your life.'
> JANE AUSTEN
> *Pride and Prejudice*

28 April 1866 When men marry they think they are marrying a particular girl with a particular character, and they don't seem to realize that it will change ... It is not so much the girl's character that matters as all the influences she undergoes during her early married life.
> COUNTESS SOPHIE TOLSTOY
> *Diary 1862–91*

When marrying, one should ask oneself this question: Do you believe that you will be able to converse well with this woman into your old age?
> NIETZSCHE
> *Human, All Too Human*

'I don't believe I shall ever marry. I'm happy as I am, and love my liberty too well to be in any hurry to give it up for any mortal man.'

    LOUISA MAY ALCOTT
    Little Women

'I pay very little regard,' said Mrs Grant, 'to what any young person says on the subject of marriage. If they profess a disinclination for it, I only set it down that they have not yet seen the right person.'

    JANE AUSTEN
    Mansfield Park

My mind is quite made up – and I told Albert this morning of it; the warm affection he showed me on learning this gave me *great* pleasure. He seems *perfection*, and I think that I have the prospect of very great happiness before me. I *love* him *more* than I can say … We also think it better, and Albert quite approves of it, that we should be married very soon after Parliament meets, about the beginning of February; and indeed, loving Albert as I do, I cannot wish it should be delayed. My feelings are a little changed, I must say, since last Spring, when I said I couldn't *think* of marrying for *three or four years*; but seeing Albert has changed all this.

    QUEEN VICTORIA
    in a letter to her Uncle Leopold, 15 October 1839

'I can make you happy,' said he ... 'You shall have a piano in a year or two – farmers' wives are getting to have pianos now – and I'll practise up the flute right well to play with you in the evenings ... And at home by the fire, whenever you look up, there I shall be – and whenever I look up, there will be you.'

THOMAS HARDY
Far from the Madding Crowd

'I lay it down as a general rule, Harriet, that if a woman *doubts* as to whether she should accept a man or not, she certainly ought to refuse him. If she can hesitate as to "Yes", she ought to say "No" directly.'

JANE AUSTEN
Emma

Ted, she felt, would stand by her, if she resolved to have the baby; maybe he would even marry her ... But she did not want to marry Ted, nor, she was certain, did he want to marry her.

MARGARET DRABBLE
The Middle Ground

'Say yes, Becky,' Sir Pitt continued. 'I'm an old man, but a good'n. I'm good for twenty years. I'll make you happy, zee if I don't. You shall do what you like; spend what you like; and 'av it all your own way. I'll make you a zettlement. I'll do everything reglar. Look year!' and the old man fell down on his knees and leered at her like a satyr.

W.M. THACKERAY
Vanity Fair

Daisy, Daisy, give me your answer, do!
I'm half crazy, all for the love of you!
It won't be a stylish marriage,
I can't afford a carriage,
But you'll look sweet upon the seat
Of a bicycle made for two!
    HARRY DACRE
    'Daisy Bell'
    late 19th century

To be accepted by you as your husband and the earthly guardian of your welfare, I should regard as the highest of providential gifts. In return, I can at least offer you an affection hitherto unwasted, and the faithful consecration of a life which, however short in the sequel, has no backward pages whereon, if you choose to turn them, you will find records such as might justly cause you either bitterness or shame.
    GEORGE ELIOT
    Mr Casaubon proposes to Dorothea in *Middlemarch*

I cannot do better than make her my wife. I will fashion her soul the way I want it; she is like a piece of wax in my hands, and I can give her the shape I like.
    MOLIÈRE
    L'Ecole des femmes

A man who marries a woman to educate her falls a victim to the same fallacy as the woman who marries a man to reform him.
    ELBERT HUBBARD
    The Note Book, 1927

'And if you would promise me to read a little – a little Cookery Book that I would send you, it would be so excellent for both of us. For our path in life, my Dora,' said I, warming with the subject, 'is stony and rugged now, and it rests with us to smooth it. We must fight our way onward. We must be brave. There are obstacles to be met, and we must meet, and crush them!'

    CHARLES DICKENS
    David Copperfield

He contemplated her absorbed young face with a thrill of possessorship in which pride in his own masculine initiation was mingled with a tender reverence for her abysmal purity. 'We'll read *Faust* together ... by the Italian lakes ... ' he thought, somewhat hazily confusing the scene of his projected honeymoon with the masterpieces of literature which it would be his manly privilege to reveal to his bride.

    EDITH WHARTON
    The Age of Innocence

And now you are to be mine! Now I am about to experience celestial joy on earth! I see you as a young wife, then a young mother, but always the same Adèle, as adoring and adored in the chastity of married life as in the virgin days of your first love.

    VICTOR HUGO
    in a letter to Adèle Foucher (to whom he was
    notoriously unfaithful), 15 March 1822, shortly
    before their marriage

She is mine to have and to hold!
She has chosen between love and gold!
All the joys life can give
Shall be hers, while I live,
For she's mine to have and to hold.
> WILL A. HEELAN
> 'She Is Mine to Have and to Hold'

His lips were very near to Araminta's as he said:

'It is my sweet, something for which all men hunger, all men long for and for which all men search. It is love – the real love which unites two people so that they become one.'

'And that ... is what has ... happened to us!'

'That is what will happen completely and irrevocably when we are married,' the Marquis promised. 'And because we have found love we are truly blessed, my Sweetheart, and we shall, I swear, be eternally happy.'
> BARBARA CARTLAND
> *Hungry for Love*

Thus hand in hand through life we'll go;
Its checkered paths of joy and woe
With cautious steps we'll tread
> NATHANIEL COTTON
> 'The Fireside'

I've sometimes thought of marrying, and then I've thought again.
> NOEL COWARD
> in 1956

I have come to the conclusion never again to think of marrying, and for this reason: I can never be satisfied with anyone who would be blockhead enough to have me.

> ABRAHAM LINCOLN
> in a letter to Mrs O.H. Browning, 1 April 1838

The men that women marry,
And why they marry them, will always be
A marvel and a mystery to the world.

> H.W. LONGFELLOW
> 'Michael Angelo'

Advice to persons about to marry – Don't.

> HENRY MAYHEW
> *Punch*, 1845

Can't you feel how certainly I love you and how certainly we shall be married? Only let us wait just a short time, to get strong again. Two shaken, rather sick people together would be a bad start. A little waiting, let us have, because I love you ... Do you know, like the old knights, I seem to want a certain time to prepare myself – a sort of vigil with myself. Because it is a great thing for me to marry you, not a quick, passionate coming together ... I am a bit awe-inspired – I want to get used to it.

> D.H. LAWRENCE
> in a letter to Frieda Lawrence, 15 May 1912

Left alone, Levin asked himself again if he really felt any regret for the freedom his friends had been talking about. The idea made him smile. 'Freedom? What do I need freedom for? Happiness for me consists in loving, in thinking Kitty's thoughts and wishing her wishes, *without* any freedom.'

Then the smile left his face. 'Do I *know* her thoughts, her wishes and feelings?' He lapsed into gloom, assailed with fear and doubt. 'What if she didn't love me? What if she was only marrying me to get married?'

> LEO TOLSTOY
> *Anna Karenina*

It was a damp disagreeable morning. Nevertheless, at twenty minutes to ten o'clock, Oak came out of his house, and

Went up the hill side
With that sort of stride
A man puts out when walking in search of a bride,

and knocked at Bathsheba's door. Ten minutes later a large and a smaller umbrella might have been seen moving from the same door, and through the mist along the road to the church. The distance was not more than a quarter of a mile, and these two sensible persons deemed it unnecessary to drive.

> THOMAS HARDY
> *Far from the Madding Crowd*

Emma would, on the contrary, have liked the wedding to take place at midnight, by torchlight.

> GUSTAVE FLAUBERT
> *Madame Bovary*

'I am off, you see – gone like a shot. Alfred and I intended to be married in this way almost from the first; we never meant to be spliced in the humdrum way of other people; Alfred has too much spirit for that, and so have I – Dieu merci!'

CHARLOTTE BRONTË
Villette

The reason for much matrimony is patrimony.

OGDEN NASH

The marriage was in the sacristy of a Catholic Church. Question of having to. They wouldn't do it out front because he was divorced and she was heavily pregnant.

EDNA O'BRIEN
Girls in Their Married Bliss

Marriage: a ceremony in which rings are put on the finger of the lady and through the nose of the gentleman.

HERBERT SPENCER
Definitions

What could be more absurd than to assemble a crowd to witness a man and a woman promising to love each other for the rest of their lives, when we know what human creatures are – men so thoroughly selfish and unprincipled, women so vain and frivolous?

EMILY EDEN
The Semi-Attached Couple, 1830

Marriage is a ghastly public confession of a strictly private intention.

IAN HAY
Scottish novelist

In a word, George had thrown the great cast. He was going to be married. Hence his pallor and nervousness – his sleepless night and agitation in the morning. I have heard people who have gone through the same thing own to the same emotion. After three or four ceremonies, you get accustomed to it, no doubt; but the first dip, everybody allows, is awful.

> W.M. THACKERAY
> *Vanity Fair*

For next to that interesting job,
The hanging of Jack, or Bill, or Bob,
There's nothing so draws a London mob
As the noosing of very rich people.

> THOMAS HOOD
> 'Miss Kilmansegg: Her Courtship'

25 December 1665   To church in the morning, and there saw a wedding in the church, which I have not seen many a day; and the young people so merry one with another, and strange to see what delight we married people have to see these poor fools decoyed into our condition, every man and woman gazing and smiling at them.

> SAMUEL PEPYS
> *Diary*

There was nobody in the church besides the officiating persons and the small marriage party and their attendants. The two valets sat aloof superciliously. The rain came rattling down on the windows. In the intervals of the service you heard it, and the sobbing of old Mrs Sedley in the pew.

> W.M. THACKERAY
> *Vanity Fair*

The day of her wedding was stifling, and in the narrow church of Saint-Clair, the chattering of the women rose above the sound of the winded old harmonium, while their various scents overpowered the smell of incense. It was then that Thérèse felt lost. She had entered the cage as if sleepwalking, and as the heavy door clanged shut behind her, the wretched child was waking up.

    FRANÇOIS MAURIAC
    Thérèse Desqueyroux

The music, the scent of the lilies on the altar, the vision of the cloud of tulle and orange-blossoms floating nearer and nearer, the sight of Mrs Archer's face suddenly convulsed with happy sobs, the low benedictory murmur of the Rector's voice, the ordered evolutions of the eight pink bridesmaids and the eight black ushers: all these sights, sounds and sensations, so familiar in themselves, so unutterably strange and meaningless in his new relation to them, were confusedly mingled in his brain.

   'My God,' he thought, '*have* I got the ring?' – and once more he went through the bridegroom's convulsive gesture.

    EDITH WHARTON
    The Age of Innocence

As for Levin, he had no eyes but for Kitty. Everybody thought she looked far less pretty than usual under her bridal crown, and far from her best; but Levin did not think so. He looked at her upswept hair, with her long white veil and white flowers, … and to him she looked more beautiful than ever.

    LEO TOLSTOY
    Anna Karenina

Hardly had the last words of the Hallelujah chorus died away in solemn echoes, when the ceremonial, as arranged by chamberlains and heralds, ended, and the bride giving vent to her evidently long pent-up feelings, turned and flung herself upon her mother's bosom with a suddenness and depth of feeling that thrilled through every heart ...

There was no mistake about the expression of the bride's face as she quitted the sacred building. Her delicate colour returned, her eyes sparkled with emotion, and there was such a light of happiness upon her features as she turned upon her Royal husband a look of the most supreme affection, that even the most reserved felt moved and an audible 'God bless her' passing from mouth to mouth accompanied her upon her way.

> description in *The Times* of the wedding of Princess Vicky (eldest child of Queen Victoria) to Prince Frederick of Prussia at St James's Palace on 26 January 1858

'Tis o'er; the holy rite is done,
The rite that 'incorporates two in one',
– And now for the feasting, and frolic, and fun!
Spare we to tell of the smiling and sighing,
The shaking of hands, the embracing, and crying ...

> R.H. BARHAM
> 'The Wedding-Day', *The Ingoldsby Legends*

Madame Bovary senior did not open her lips all day. She had been consulted neither over her daughter-in-law's dress, nor over the arrangements for the wedding feast; she left early.

> GUSTAVE FLAUBERT
> *Madame Bovary*

'Write to me very often, my dear.'

'As often as I can. But you know married women have never much time for writing. My sisters may write to *me*. They will have nothing else to do.'

> JANE AUSTEN
> *Pride and Prejudice*

Fancy caused her looks to wear as much matronly expression as was obtainable out of six hours' experience as a wife, in order that the contrast between her own state of life and that of the unmarried young women present might be duly impressed upon the company: occasionally stealing glances of admiration at her left hand ...

> THOMAS HARDY
> *Under the Greenwood Tree*

As the bridegroom rejoiceth over the bride ...

> ISAIAH, 62:5

Solon bade the bride eat a quince the first night of marriage, intimating thereby, it seems, that the bridegroom was to expect his first pleasure from the bride's mouth and conversation.

> PLUTARCH
> *Morals: Conjugal Precepts*

Need we expose to vulgar sight
The raptures of the bridal night? ...
Let it suffice, that each had charms;
He clasp'd a goddess in his arms;
And, though she felt his usage rough,
Yet in a man 'twas well enough.

> OLIVER GOLDSMITH
> 'The Double Transformation'

47

I write to you from here, the happiest, happiest Being that ever existed. Really, I do not think it *possible* for any one in the world to be *happier*, or as happy as I am. He is an Angel, and his kindness and affection for me is really touching. To look in those dear eyes, and that dear sunny face, is enough to make me adore him. What I can do to make him happy will be my greatest delight.

> QUEEN VICTORIA
> in a letter from Windsor to her Uncle Leopold, 11 February 1840, the day after her wedding to Albert

It was difficult not to be introspective on our honeymoon. Besides, Venice turned out not to be the ideal location, for I was suffering from a late bout of morning sickness ... A gondola was particular torture.

> RACHEL BILLINGTON
> *A Woman's Age*

... Henry, surfeiting in joys of love, with his new bride ...

> SHAKESPEARE
> *Henry VI*, Part 2

And it happened that Erec loved Enid with such passion that he forgot all about knightly preoccupations and failed to go to tournaments. All he wanted to do was spend his time in amorous dalliance with his wife ..., often lying in bed with her till after midday, and then idling the day long in kisses and caresses. His companions were mortified.

> CHRÉTIEN DE TROYES
> *Erec et Enide*, 12th century

In house to kepe housholde,
whan folks wyll wed,
Mo thyngs belong,
than foure bare legs in a bed.
    JOHN HEYWOOD
    Dialogue

Nought now was heard, but Love and Dear,
My Dear go there! My Love come here!
And, since it is such charming weather,
O let us take a stroll together;
While she would sing to some fine tune,
'Our life shall be one honeymoon'.
    WILLIAM COMBE
    The Third Tour of Dr Syntax, in Search of a Wife, 1821

Nothing is to me more distasteful than that entire complacency and satisfaction which beam in the countenances of a new-married couple – in that of the lady particularly; it tells you, that her lot is disposed of in this world; that *you* can have no hopes of her. It is true, I have none; nor wishes either, perhaps ... But what I have spoken of is nothing to the airs which these creatures give themselves when they come, as they generally do, to have children.
    CHARLES LAMB
    Essays of Elia

The first seven months of their marriage was more like blue sky than brown earth; and if any one had told Mabel that her husband was a mortal, and not an angel, sent to her that her days and nights might be unmixed, uninterrupted heaven, she could hardly have realised the information.

CHARLES READE
Peg Woffington

Clym and Eustacia, in their little house at Alderworth, were living on with a monotony which was delightful to them. The heath and changes of weather were quite blotted out from their eyes for the present ... When it rained they were charmed, because they could remain indoors together all day with such a show of reason; when it was fine they were charmed, because they could sit together on the hills ... The absolute solitude in which they lived intensified their reciprocal thoughts; yet some might have said that it had the disadvantage of consuming their mutual affections at a fearfully prodigal rate.

THOMAS HARDY
The Return of the Native

Is there anything more attractive to the newly married Benedick than the cosiness of his evenings at home, ... by the side of his sweet partner for life? Even though she objects to his putting his boots on the sofa or badgers him into wearing a swallow-tail coat at dinner every night, is he not a thousand-fold happier than when flitting from ball-room to theatre and from theatre to club in search of feverish excitement?

ROBERT GRANT
Reflections of a Married Man, 1892

Marriage is a book of which the first chapter is written in poetry and the remaining chapters in prose.
BEVERLEY NICHOLS

Marriage is a meal where the soup is better than the dessert.
AUSTIN O'MALLEY
American writer

They perceived that the love, unceasing and ecstatic, of which they had dreamt before their union, was a chimera existing only in imagination; and they awoke, with sobered feelings, to seek content in rational affection ...: each acknowledging, with a sigh, that even in a marriage of love, the brilliant anticipations of imagination are never realised; that disappointment awaits poor mortals even in that brightest portion of existence – The Honey-Moon.
MARGUERITE BLESSINGTON
'The Honey-Moon', *The Works of Lady Blessington*, 1838

'Yes, I fear we are cooling – I see it as well as you,' she sighed mournfully. 'And how madly we loved two months ago! You were never tired of contemplating me, nor I of contemplating you. Who could have thought then that by this time my eyes would not seem so very bright to yours, nor your lips so very sweet to mine? Two months – is it possible? Yes, 'tis too true.'
THOMAS HARDY
The Return of the Native

A dish o' married love grows soon cauld.
SCOTTISH PROVERB

I have seen marriages where, at first, husband and wife seemed as though they would eat one another up; in six months they have separated in mutual disgust. 'Tis the Devil inspires this evanescent ardour, in order to divert the parties from prayer.

MARTIN LUTHER
Table-Talk

When a couple are newly-married, the first month is honey-moon or smick smack; the second is hither and thither; the third is thwick thwack; the fourth, the Devil take them that brought thee and I together.

JOHN RAY
English Proverbs

Henry had, indeed, ceased to regard his wife with the ardour of romantic passion; nor had the solid feelings of affectionate esteem supplied its place: but he loved her still, because he believed himself the engrossing object of her tenderness; and, in that blest delusion, he had hitherto found palliatives for her folly, and consolation for all his own distresses.

SUSAN FERRIER
Marriage, 1818

Before her marriage, Emma had taken what she felt to be love; but the happiness which should have been hers had not materialized, and she must therefore have mistaken her feelings, she thought. And Emma wondered what was meant in life by the words bliss, passion and ecstasy, which had seemed so exalted in books.

GUSTAVE FLAUBERT
Madame Bovary

Marriage from Love, like vinegar from wine –
A sad, sour, sober beverage – by Time
Is sharpened from its high celestial flavour
Down to a very homely household savour.
    BYRON
    Don Juan

Romola's touch and glance no longer stirred any fibre of tenderness in her husband. The good-humoured, tolerant Tito, ... disposed always to be gentle towards the rest of the world, felt himself becoming strangely hard towards this wife whose presence had once been the strongest influence he had known.
    GEORGE ELIOT
    Romola

Men are always doomed to be duped ... They are always wooing goddesses, and marrying mere mortals.
    WASHINGTON IRVING
    Bracebridge Hall

But when a twelvemonth pass'd away,
Jack found his goddess made of clay;
Found half the charms that deck'd her face
Arose from powder, shreds, and lace;
But still the worst remain'd behind,
That very face had robb'd her mind.
    OLIVER GOLDSMITH
    'The Double Transformation'

Keep your eyes wide open before marriage, and half-shut afterwards.
    BENJAMIN FRANKLIN
    Poor Richard

Mark was a Pill. His little Dame had Class ...
One of those Unions that neglect to Une ...
She was a Saint! He was a Hound! Alas,
That such a Peach should marry such a Prune!
  DON MARQUIS
  Tristram and Isolt

Zounds! madam, you had no taste when you married me!
  RICHARD BRINSLEY SHERIDAN
  The School for Scandal

The first sign that things are amiss between the two who
thought they were entering paradise together, is generally a
sense of loneliness, a feeling that the one who was expected
to have all in common is outside some experience, some
subtle delight, and fails to understand the needs of the
loved one. Trivialities are often the first indicators of
something which takes its roots unseen in the profoundest
depths.
  MARIE STOPES
  Married Love, 1918

The old unhappy feeling pervaded my life. It was deepened,
if it were changed at all; but it was as undefined as ever, and
addressed me like a strain of sorrowful music faintly heard
in the night. I loved my wife dearly, and I was happy; but
the happiness I had vaguely anticipated, once, was not the
happiness I enjoyed, and there was always something
wanting.
  CHARLES DICKENS
  David Copperfield

But the absolutely extraordinary thing was that he hadn't the slightest idea that Isabel wasn't as happy as he. God, what blindness! He hadn't the remotest notion in those days that she really hated that inconvenient little house, that she thought the fat Nanny was ruining the babies, that she was desperately lonely, pining for new people and new music and pictures and so on.

> KATHARINE MANSFIELD
> *Marriage à la Mode*

James, being a quiet, fireside, perusing man, felt at times a wide gap between himself and Olive, his wife, who loved riding and driving and outdoor jaunts to a degree; while Steve, who was always knocking about hither and thither, had a very domestic wife, who worked samplers, and made hearthrugs, scarcely ever wished to cross the threshold, and only drove out with him to please him.

> THOMAS HARDY
> *Life's Little Ironies*

To marry is to learn to be alone.

> FRENCH PROVERB

A good marriage is that in which each appoints the other guardian of his solitude.

> RAINER MARIA RILKE

A good marriage is one which allows for change and growth in the individuals.

> PEARL BUCK
> *To My Daughters, with Love*

It usually takes some time for the husband and wife to know each other's humours and habits, and to find what surrender of their own they can make with the least reluctance for their mutual good.

> AMELIA OPIE
> *A Wife's Duty*

Marriage is a science.

> HONORÉ DE BALZAC
> *Physiologie du mariage*

'There can be no disparity in marriage, like unsuitability of mind and purpose.' Those words I remembered too. I had endeavoured to adapt Dora to myself, and found it impracticable. It remained for me to adapt myself to Dora; to share with her what I could, and be happy; to bear on my own shoulders what I must, and be happy still. This was the discipline to which I tried to bring my heart, when I began to think. It made my second year much happier than my first; and, what was better still, made Dora's life all sunshine.

> CHARLES DICKENS
> *David Copperfield*

So far from becoming a cowboy, or a satrap, or the President of the Republic, or a billionaire, or a bushman, he has reconciled himself to the idea of plodding along in a rut at home, unillumined even by the hope of stopping a runaway horse. With the consciousness of the mortgage on his little house fresh in mind, and the prospect of a larger family staring him in the face, he recognizes that the chances are against his ever seeing an ostrich farm or a

dance of dervishes ... In other words, he has become a fixture; part and parcel of his own environment, and hopelessly entangled with the butcher, the baker, the candlestick-maker, the plumber, the school-teacher, the physician and the clergyman.

ROBERT GRANT
Reflections of a Married Man, 1892

But marriage, if comfortable, is not at all heroic. It certainly narrows and dampens the spirits of generous men. In marriage, a man becomes slack and selfish, and undergoes a fatty degeneration of his moral being. The air of the fireside withers out all the fine wildings of the husband's heart.

ROBERT LOUIS STEVENSON
Virginibus Puerisque

He is dreadfully married. He's the most married man I ever saw in my life.

ARTEMUS WARD
A Mormon Romance

A married man forms married habits and becomes dependent on marriage just as a sailor becomes dependent on the sea.

GEORGE BERNARD SHAW

Marriage must constantly fight against a monster which devours everything: routine.

HONORÉ DE BALZAC
Physiologie du mariage

In courtship everything is regarded as provisional and preliminary, and the smallest sample of virtue or accomplishment is taken to guarantee delightful stores which the broad leisure of marriage will reveal. But the door-sill of marriage once crossed, expectation is concentrated on the present. Having once embarked on your marital voyage, it is impossible not to be aware that you make no way and that the sea is not within sight – that, in fact, you are exploring an enclosed basin.

> GEORGE ELIOT
> *Middlemarch*

Love cannot exist in marriage, because love is an ideal: that is to say, something not quite understood … But a wife – you know all about her – who her father was, who her mother was, what she thinks of you and her opinion of the neighbours over the way.

> GEORGE MOORE
> *Confessions of a Young Man*, 1888

Olinda: This marrying I do not like: 'tis like going on a long voyage to sea, where after a while even the calms are distasteful, and the storms dangerous: one seldom sees a new object, 'tis still a deal of sea, sea; husband, husband, every day – till one's quite cloyed with it.

> APHRA BEHN
> *The Dutch Lover*

I have got nothing against monsieur de Fischtaminel: he doesn't gamble, he doesn't run after women, he doesn't drink, he doesn't have any ruinous tastes; as you say, he has all the negative qualities which makes husbands tolerable.

So what is the trouble? Well, mother dear, he is completely idle. We are together the whole blessed day ... Two convicts chained to the same ball are not bored for they have their escape to think about, but we do not have a single topic of conversation. We have said everything there is to say. He was, a short while ago, reduced to talking about politics, but the subject is now exhausted.

> HONORÉ DE BALZAC
> Caroline writes to her mother in *Petites Misères de la vie conjugale*

He observed, that a man of sense and education should meet a suitable companion in a wife. It was a miserable thing when the conversation could only be such as, whether the mutton should be boiled or roasted, and probably a dispute about that.

> JAMES BOSWELL
> *Life of Johnson*

A husband and wife who are both gourmands have, at least once a day, an agreeable occasion to get together. For even those who sleep apart (and there are many of them) usually eat at the same table; and they then have an ever renewable subject of conversation: what they are eating, what they have eaten, and what they are going to eat.

> BRILLAT-SAVARIN
> *La Physiologie du goût*

What is it, ladies, that so often drives out men to clubs, and leaves the domestic hearth desolate – what but bad dinners? And whose fault is the bad dinners but yours – yours, forsooth, who are too intellectual to go into the kitchen, and too delicate to think about your husband's victuals? I know a case in which the misery of a whole life ... arose from a wife's high and mightly neglect of the good things of life, where ennui, estrangement, and subsequent ruin and suicide arose out of an obstinate practice of serving a leg of mutton three days running ... Where the mutton is habitually cold in a house, depend on it the affection grows cold too.

> W.M. THACKERAY
> *Miscellaneous Papers*

Feed the brute.

> GEORGE DU MAURIER
> advice given in *Punch* for keeping a husband's love, 1886

'I suspect she could endure existence even upon roast mutton, with the man she loves.'

'That's nothing to the purpose, unless the man she loves, as you call it, loves to live upon roast mutton too. Take my word for it, unless she gives her husband good dinners, he'll not care twopence for her in a week's time. I look upon bad dinners to be the source of much of the misery we hear of in the married life. Women are much mistaken, if they think it's by dressing themselves they are to please their husbands.'

> SUSAN FERRIER
> *Marriage*, 1818

Who invented that mischievous falsehood that the way to a man's heart was through his stomach? How many a silly woman, taking it for truth, has let love slip out of the parlour while she was busy in the kitchen … A moderately cooked dinner – let us say a not-too-well cooked dinner, with you looking your best … makes a pleasanter meal for us, after the day's work is done, than that same dinner, cooked to perfection, with you silent, jaded, and anxious, your pretty hair untidy, your pretty face wrinkled with care concerning the sole, with anxiety regarding the omelette.

> JEROME K. JEROME
> *The Second Thoughts of an Idle Fellow*

The truth was that Cunégonde was really rather ugly; but her pastry was outstanding.

> VOLTAIRE
> *Candide, ou l'Optimisme*

Very few people that have settled entirely in the country, but have grown at length weary of one another. The lady's conversation generally falls into a thousand impertinent effects of idleness; and the gentleman falls in love with his dogs and his horses, and out of love with everything else.

> LADY MARY WORTLEY MONTAGU
> in a letter to Edward Wortley Montagu, shortly
> before their marriage in August 1712

Husband and wife come to look alike at last.

> OLIVER WENDELL HOLMES
> *The Professor at the Breakfast-Table*

… that moral centaur, man and wife …

> BYRON
> *Don Juan*

Most iv th' ol' marrid men I know threat their wives like a rockin'-chair, a great comfort whin they're tired, but apt to be in th' way at other times.

FINLEY PETER DUNNE
Dissertations by Mr Dooley, 1906

'I am your wife, and why will you not listen? Yes, I am your wife indeed.'

'I know what that tone means.'

'What tone?'

'The tone in which you said, "Your wife indeed". It meant, "Your wife, worse luck".'

THOMAS HARDY
The Return of the Native

Erica knows that Brian knows what she is thinking about, and he knows she knows he knows ... But if he asks what she is thinking, she will not admit it.

ALISON LURIE
The War Between the Tates

'Whatever you say.'

'Whatever *you* say,' he corrected her.

DOROTHY PARKER
Too Bad

Whenever a husband and wife begin to discuss their marriage, they are giving evidence at an inquest.

H.L. MENCKEN

'Why did you marry me?'

'I married ... a background, I suppose.'

'What do you think about marriage?'

'I don't think it exists, really. There are just human beings in situations they make for themselves.'

> PENELOPE MORTIMER
> *The Pumpkin Eater*

It is not marriage that fails; it is people that fail. All that marriage does is to show people up.

> HARRY EMERSON FOSDICK
> *Marriage*

'I see he's in favor iv short-term marredges.'

'What d'ye mean?' asked Mr Dooley. 'Reducin' th' terms f'r good behavyor?'

'No,' said Mr Hennessy. 'He says people ought to get marrid f'r three or four years at a time. Thin, if they don't like each other, or if wan gets tired, they break up housekeepin'.'

'Well,' said Mr Dooley, 'it mightn't be a bad thing. Th' trouble about mathrimony, as I have obsarved it fr'm me seat in th' gran' stand, is that afther fifteen or twinty years it settles down to an endurance thrile.

> FINLEY PETER DUNNE
> *Dissertations by Mr Dooley*, 1906

16 December 1890 The very thought of all the things which fill all my waking hours is overwhelming – the children's lessons and illnesses, my husband's health and morale ..., the sale of the Samara estate and the plans and documents I have to copy for the buyers, proofs of volume 13, which contains the banned *Kreutzer Sonata*, for the new

edition, the lawsuit against the Ovsiannikovo priest, ...
household expenses, insurance, land taxes, accounts to be
kept and copied, it seems endless.

> COUNTESS SOPHIE TOLSTOY
> *Diary 1862–91*

Our family life never was normal or well regulated. Instead
there were constant states of alert as we rescued the
children and ourselves from dangers real and imaginary.
But that is how it is in most families.

> LEO TOLSTOY
> *The Kreutzer Sonata*

Give up all hope of peace so long as your mother-in-law is
alive.

> JUVENAL
> *Satires*

In the blithe days of honey-moon,
With Kate's allurements smitten,
I lov'd her late, I lov'd her soon,
And call'd her dearest kitten.

But now my kitten's grown a cat,
And cross like other wives,
O! by my soul, my honest Mat,
I fear she has nine lives.

> quoted by JAMES BOSWELL in *Life of Johnson*

I'm sure I don't know who'd be a poor woman! I don't know
who'd tie themselves up to a man, if they knew only half
they'd have to bear. A wife must stay at home, and be a

drudge, whilst a man can go anywhere. It's enough for a wife to sit like Cinderella by the ashes, whilst her husband can go drinking and singing at a tavern. *You never sing?* How do I know you never sing? It's very well for you to say so; but if I could hear you, I daresay you're among the worst of 'em ...

Faugh! Pah! Whewgh! That filthy tobacco smoke! It's enough to kill any decent woman. You know I hate tobacco, and yet you will do it. *You don't smoke yourself?* What of that? If you go among people who *do* smoke, you're just as bad, or worse.

    DOUGLAS JERROLD
    Mrs Caudle's Curtain Lectures, 1846

Choose a wife rather by your ear than your eye.

    THOMAS FULLER
    Gnomologia, 1732

Better to sit up all night than to go to bed with a dragon.

    JEREMY TAYLOR
    The Rule and Exercises of Holy Living, 1650

Man's best possession is a sympathetic wife.

    EURIPIDES
    Antigone

Well, if a woman hadn't better be in her grave than be married! That is, if she can't be married to a decent man. No; I don't care if you are tired, I *shan't* let you go to sleep. No, and I won't say what I have to say in the morning; I'll say it now. It's all very well for you to come home at what time you like – it's now half-past twelve – and expect I'm to hold my tongue, and let you go to sleep ...

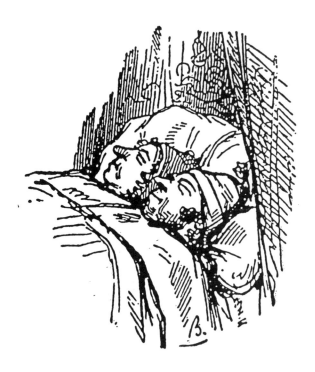

How any decent man can go and spend his nights in a tavern! – oh yes, Mr Caudle, I daresay you *do* go for rational conversation. I should like to know how many of you would care for what you call rational conversation, if you had it without your filthy brandy-and-water; yes, and your more filthy tobacco-smoke. I'm sure the last time you came home, I had the headache for a week.

> DOUGLAS JERROLD
> *Mrs Caudle's Curtain Lectures*, 1846

Before marriage, a man will lie awake all night thinking about something you said; after marriage, he'll fall asleep before you finish saying it.

> HELEN ROWLAND
> American columnist

How much the wife is dearer than the bride.

> GEORGE LYTTELTON
> 'An Irregular Ode'

At dinner, between the first and the second course, the conversation turned to marital happiness.

'There is nothing easier for a woman than to be happy,' said Caroline ...

'Do tell us your secret, madame,' said monsieur de Fischtaminel eagerly.

'A woman only has to mind her own business, consider herself the number one servant in the household, or possibly the master's personal slave, to have no wishes and express no opinions; then all is well.'

She spoke in a tearful voice, full of resentment. Adolphe stared at his wife, aghast.

> HONORÉ DE BALZAC
> *Philosophie de la vie conjugale*

A man's wife has more power over him than the state has.

> RALPH WALDO EMERSON
> *Journals*

Manny a man that cud rule a hundherd millyon sthrangers with an ir'n hand is careful to take off his shoes in th' front hallway whin he comes home late at night.

> FINLEY PETER DUNNE
> *Mr Dooley on Making a Will*, 1919

Those men are most apt to be obsequious and conciliating abroad who are under the discipline of shrews at home.

> WASHINGTON IRVING
> *The Sketch Book of Geoffrey Crayon, Gent.*

He had by heart the whole detail of woe
Xantippe made her good man undergo;
How oft she scolded in a day he knew,
How many pisspots on the sage she threw –
Who took it patiently, and wiped his head:
'Rain follows thunder,' that was all he said.

> GEOFFREY CHAUCER
> *The Wife of Bath*
> on the sufferings of Socrates, king of the hen-pecked
> translated by Alexander Pope

71

It's my old girl that advises. She has the head. But I never own to it before her. Discipline must be maintained.

CHARLES DICKENS
Bleak House

Caudle, love, do you know what next Sunday is? *No! you don't?*

Well, was there ever such a strange man! Can't you guess, darling? Next Sunday, dear? Think, love, a minute – just think.

What! and you don't know now?

Ha! if I hadn't a better memory than you, I don't know how we should ever get on. Well, then, pet – shall I tell you what next Sunday is? Why, then, it's our wedding-day – What are you groaning at, Mr Caudle? I don't see anything to groan at. If anybody should groan, I'm sure it isn't you. No, I rather think it's I who ought to groan!

Oh, dear! That's fourteen years ago. You were a very different man then, Mr Caudle. What do you say –? *And I was a very different woman?* Not at all – just the same.

DOUGLAS JERROLD
Mrs Caudle's Curtain Lectures, 1846

'Don't ye know what this is?' says she.

'Sure,' says he, 'it's Choosdah.'

'No, but what day?'

'I give it up. St Pathrick's day, Valentine's day, pay day. What's th' answer?'

'But think.'

'I give it up.'

'It's th' annyvarsary iv our weddin'.'

'Oh,' says he, 'so it is. I'd clean f'rgot. That's right. I raymimber it well, now that ye mintion it. Well, betther luck nex' time.'

FINLEY PETER DUNNE
Dissertations by Mr Dooley, 1906

Marriage is the alliance of two people, one of whom never remembers birthdays and the other never forgets them.

OGDEN NASH

You may think you had a conscience, but what is a conscience to a wife? ... To marry is to domesticate the Recording Angel.

ROBERT LOUIS STEVENSON
Virginibus Puerisque

Marriage is like pleading guilty to an indefinite sentence. Without parole.

JOHN MORTIMER
The Trials of Rumpole

There isn't a wife in the world who has not taken the exact measure of her husband, weighed him and settled him in her own mind, and knows him as well as if she had ordered him after designs and specifications of her own.

CHARLES DUDLEY WARNER
Backlog Studies

Who says that Giles and Joan at discord be?
The observing neighbours no such mood can see.
Indeed, poor Giles repents he married ever.
But that his Joan doth too. And Giles would never,
By his free will, be in Joan's company.
No more would Joan he should. Giles riseth early,
And having got him out of doors is glad.
The like is Joan. But turning home, is sad.
And so is Joan …
　　BEN JONSON
　　'On Giles and Joan'

Sganarelle: Oh what a tiresome thing it is to have a wife! And how right Aristotle was to say a woman's worse than a demon …
Martine: Cursed be the day and hour when I was ill advised enough to say yes!
Sganarelle: Cursed be the horn beak of a notary who made me sign my ruin! … Sweet object of my dreams, I'll warm your ears.
Martine: You drunkard!
Sganarelle: I'll lather you.
Martine: You wine bag!
　　MOLIÈRE
　　Le Médecin malgré lui

The best thing a woman can do is to marry. It appears to me that even quarrels with one's husband are preferable to the ennui of a solitary existence.
　　ELIZABETH PATTERSON BONAPARTE
　　in a letter to Lady Charles Morgan, 11 August 1817

'You're a brute,' she continued, not heeding him, obsessed by her own wound. 'You're a brute!' She said it with terrifying conviction. 'Everybody knows it … You're a brute and a bully …

'I think you ought to apologize to me,' she blubbered. 'Yes, I really do.'

'Why should I apologize to you? You moved the furniture against my wish. I moved it against yours. That's all. You began. I didn't begin. You want everything your own way. Well, you won't have it.'

ARNOLD BENNETT
These Twain

Still frowning, she moved chastely in beside him: for the fact that they were annoyed with each other made the act of getting naked into bed on a level with sitting beside him at breakfast.

DORIS LESSING
A Proper Marriage

All married couples should learn the art of battle as they should learn the art of making love … Good battle is healthy and constructive, and brings to a marriage the principle of equal partnership.

ANN LANDERS
American columnist

Their married life has been one carnal, bloody fight.

D.H. LAWRENCE
writing of his parents' marriage, in a letter to Rachel Annand Taylor, 3 December 1910

Nevertheless, there was a state of peace in the house for some time. Mrs Morel was more tolerant of him and he, depending on her almost like a child, was rather happy. Neither knew that she was more tolerant because she loved him less. Up till this time, in spite of all, he had been her husband and her man. She had felt that, more or less, what he did to himself he did to her. Her living depended on him. There were many stages in the ebbing of her love for him, but it was always ebbing.

> D.H. LAWRENCE
> *Sons and Lovers*

The strained and precarious relationship between Ann and Randall ... was also a constant source of pain and surprise ... It seemed to him scarcely credible that two married people could continue on such terms, being so cold and mysterious to each other and so *silent*.

> IRIS MURDOCH
> *An Unofficial Rose*

Body and soul, like peevish man and wife,
United jar, and yet are loath to part.

> EDWARD YOUNG
> *Night Thoughts*

I have known many happy marriages, but never a compatible one. The whole aim of marriage is to fight through and survive the instant when incompatibility becomes unquestionable. For a man and a woman, as such, are incompatible.

> G.K. CHESTERTON
> *What's Wrong with the World*

The one charm of marriage is that it makes a life of deception absolutely necessary for both parties.

> OSCAR WILDE
> *The Picture of Dorian Gray*

Marriage is an arrangement by which two people start by getting the best out of each other and often end by getting the worst.

> GERALD BRENAN
> *Thoughts in a Dry Season*

Marriage means expectations and expectations mean conflict.

> ANTHONY CLARE
> writing in *The Sunday Times*, March 1990

Marriage is a status of antagonistic cooperation.

> JOHN M. WOOLSEY
> federal judge, in 1931

Marriage is no marriage that is not basically and permanently phallic, and that is not linked up with the sun and the earth, the moon and the fixed stars and the planets.

> D.H. LAWRENCE
> *A Propos of Lady Chatterley's Lover*

14 December 1890   I copied Lyova's diaries up to the point where he says: 'There is no love; there is only the physical need for intercourse, and the rational need for a life companion.' If I had known this was his view twenty-nine years ago, I would never have married him.

> COUNTESS SOPHIE TOLSTOY
> *Diary 1862–91*

The total amount of undesired sex endured by women is probably greater in marriage than in prostitution.
> BERTRAND RUSSELL
> *Marriage and Morals*

For the first time in her life Bertha Young desired her husband. Oh, she'd loved him – she'd been in love with him, of course, in every other way, but just not in that way. And, equally, of course she'd understood that he was different. They'd discussed it so often. It had worried her dreadfully at first to find that she was so cold, but after a time it had not seemed to matter.
> KATHERINE MANSFIELD
> *Bliss*, in which the heroine is about to discover that it *does* matter

Sir, a man will not, once in a hundred instances, leave his wife and go to a harlot, if his wife has not been negligent of pleasing.
> SAMUEL JOHNSON
> Boswell's *Life of Johnson*

Lucinda: Once a Week! I wou'd not for the World bed with you oftener; why 'tis not the Fashion, Sir Toby.
> SUSANNAH CENTLIVRE
> *Love's Contrivance*, 1703

It is mostly in bed that the vapours come in useful. A woman has her vapours whenever she doesn't have migraine; when she has neither vapours nor migraine, she is under the protection of the belt of Venus.
> HONORÉ DE BALZAC
> *Physiologie du mariage*

Wedlock – the deep, deep peace of the double bed after the hurly-burly of the chaise-longue.

    MRS PATRICK CAMPBELL

Ethel and Bernard returned from their Honymoon with a son and hair a nice fat baby called Ignatius Bernard. They soon had six more children four boys and three girls and some of them were twins which was very exciting.

    DAISY ASHFORD
    The Young Visiters

Natasha had married in the early spring of 1813, and by 1820 she already had three daughters and one much wanted son whom she breastfed herself. She had filled out so much it was hard to recognize the former slender, lively Natasha in her matronly form. Her features had become firmer, and in her expression of peaceful serenity there was none of the constant fire and animation which had been her greatest charm ... She looked like a strong, fine and productive hen.

    LEO TOLSTOY
    War and Peace

I need not say any more about the basic impossibility of combining matrimony and scholarship ... Just when you are immersed in your theological or philosophical ideas, the infants begin to squall and the wet nurses try to soothe them with their monotonous crooning ... Can your attention remain undivided?

    HÉLOISE
    quoted in Abelard's *Historia Calamitatum*, 12th
    century

He that hath wife and children hath given hostages to fortune; for they are impediments to great enterprizes, either of virtue or mischief. Certainly the best works, and of greatest merit for the public, have proceeded from the unmarried or childless men.

>FRANCIS BACON
>*Of Marriage and the Single Life*

The trouble with marriage is that, while every woman is at heart a mother, every man is at heart a bachelor.

>EDWARD VERRALL LUCAS
>English essayist

That day marked the end of my romance with my husband, my old love remaining a cherished memory of what would never return. But a new feeling of love for my children, and for the father of my children, formed the basis of another happy, though entirely different, life.

>LEO TOLSTOY
>*A Happy Married Life*

His wife was casting him off, half regretfully, but relentlessly; casting him off and turning now for love and life to the children. Henceforward he was more or less a husk. And he half acquiesced, as so many men do, yielding their place to their children.

>D.H. LAWRENCE
>*Sons and Lovers*

O cultivate the nuptial soil
With fond affection's anxious toil;
Where, if love's fragrant flowers you sow,
Nor Thorns nor Horns will ever grow.
> WILLIAM COMBE
> *The Third Tour of Dr Syntax, in Search of a Wife*, 1821

My friend, I am married, and you will be soon. Write in your brain, with a steel-pen, the dictum that every married man is in danger of being made a cuckold. Cuckoldry follows marriage as naturally as the shadow follows the body.
> RABELAIS
> *Pantagruel*

Who hath a fair wife needs more than two eyes.
> JOHN RAY
> *English Proverbs*

At Rimini there lived a merchant, a man of great property, goods and wealth, who had a most beautiful wife and was inordinately jealous of her, ... imagining every man to be in love with her. He accordingly kept so close a watch over her ... that she dared not so much as show herself at a window ... She found her dismal life all the harder to bear because she knew herself to be innocent, and she cast about for a way of consoling herself which would justify his bad treatment of her.
> BOCCACCIO
> *The Decameron*

Claudine: I hate suspicious husbands, and I want mine to be so sure of my chastity that he could see me surrounded by thirty men without anxiety.
MOLIÈRE
Georges Dandin

O curse of marriage!
That we can call these delicate creatures ours,
And not their appetites. I had rather be a toad,
And live upon the vapour of a dungeon
Than keep a corner in the thing I love
For others' uses.
SHAKESPEARE
Othello

You are my wife and I love you as a mistress, and I have the torment of seeing you love another man.
Mme DE LA FAYETTE
La Princess de Clèves

It was with inexpressible pain that she realized that the feelings she had for M de Nemours, which she had hardly dared admit even to herself, were the very ones that M de Clèves had asked of her; and she thought how shameful it was that they should not go to a husband who deserved them so well but to another man.
Mme DE LA FAYETTE
La Princesse de Clèves

Loved and respected by a husband I love and respect, my duties and my pleasures are combined. I am happy, and I ought to be. If there exist more acute pleasures I do not want to know them. Is there a sweeter pleasure than to be at peace with oneself? … What you call happiness is but a turmoil of the senses, a tempest of passions which it is frightening to witness even from the safety of the shore … How would I dare embark on a sea littered with the debris of thousands of wrecks? And with whom? No, Monsieur, I prefer to remain on the shore.

> CHODERLOS DE LACLOS
> *Les Liaisons dangereuses*
> Mme de Tourvel writes to the vicomte de Valmont

'I do not have the right to pry into your feelings, and in any case consider it a fruitless and even harmful exercise,' Alexei Alexandrovich began. 'By delving into our souls, we often bring to light what could have remained undisturbed. Your feelings are a matter for your conscience; but it is my duty to you, to myself and to God to remind you of your responsibilities. Our lives are tied, not by people but by God.'

> LEO TOLSTOY
> Karenin warns his wife in *Anna Karenina*

25 October, Lords Day, 1668 My wife, coming up suddenly, did find me imbracing the girl con my hand sub su coats … I was at a wonderful loss upon it, and the girl also; and I endeavoured to put it off, but my wife was struck mute and grew angry.

> SAMUEL PEPYS
> *Diary*

She inspected all his garments for signs of infidelity – lipstick, strange hairs, semen – but found nothing. No notes in the pockets of his suits, no jewelled clips caught in his vests. Seb was so neat and clever, she reflected with a prideful hatred.

ALICE THOMAS ELLIS
The Birds of the Air

I never was in bed with my husband but I wished myself in the arms of his brother; and though his brother never offered me the least kindness that way after our marriage, but carried it just as a brother ought to do, yet it was impossible for me to do so to him; in short, I committed adultery and incest with him every day in my desires, which, without doubt, was as effectually criminal in the nature of the guilt as if I had actually done it.

DANIEL DEFOE
Moll Flanders

'I've got a lover, I've got a lover,' she repeated to herself with delight. She was at last going to know the joys of love, the fever of happiness which had eluded her. Her life would be filled with passion, ecstasy and delirium ... She remembered the heroines of books she had read, and the lyrical legion of these adulterous women began to sing in her memory with sisterly voices.

GUSTAVE FLAUBERT
Madame Bovary

'No, you have not made a mistake,' she said slowly, looking with dread at his cold expression. 'You have not made a mistake. I have been, and continue to be in despair. I hear what you say but my mind is filled with him. I love him, I'm his mistress. I cannot bear you, I'm afraid of you, I hate you … Do with me what you will.'

LEO TOLSTOY
Anna Karenina

'So you've come back,' he repeated.

She never looked up, and never spoke, the firelight playing over her motionless figure.

Suddenly she tried to rise, but he prevented her; it was then that he understood.

She had come back like an animal wounded to death, not knowing where to turn, not knowing what she was doing. The sight of her figure, huddled in the fur, was enough.

He knew then for certain that Bosinney had been her lover; knew that she had seen the report of his death – perhaps, like himself, had bought a paper at the draughty corner of a street, and read it.

JOHN GALSWORTHY
A Man of Property

'Oh yes! you are beautiful, you are gifted, and the eyes of thousands wait upon your every word and look. What wonder that he, ardent, refined, and genial, should lay his heart at your feet? And I have nothing but my love to make him love me … Oh, give him back to me! What is one heart more to you? You are so rich, and I am so poor, that without his love I have nothing, and can do nothing but sit me down and cry till my heart breaks. Give him back to me, beautiful, terrible woman! for, with all your gifts, you cannot love him as his poor Mabel does.'

> CHARLES READE
> *Peg Woffington*

So, at dinner, he told her all about Marina. He told it humbly, as an escapade that he was now ashamed of, but at the time had been too weak to resist. It wasn't that he cared for her, he said more than once.

> ELIZABETH JANE HOWARD
> *Odd Girl Out*

Why do people stay together? Putting aside 'for the sake of the children', and 'the habit of years' and 'economic reasons' as lawyers' nonsense – it's not much more – ... it's because they can't; they are bound. And nobody on earth knows what are the bonds that bind them except those two.

> KATHERINE MANSFIELD
> *A Married Man's Story*

All around her she seemed to see marriages threatened, broken, violated, marriages that were not really marriages, marriages in which deceit was commonplace and nobody thought anything of it.

> MARGARET FORSTER
> *Marital Rites*

Our bourgeois, not content with having the wives and daughters of the proletarians at their disposal, not to speak of common prostitutes, take the greatest pleasure in seducing one another's wives. Bourgeois marriage is in reality a system of wives in common.

> KARL MARX
> *The Communist Manifesto*

'To think of the Weldons separating! Why, I always used to say to Jim, 'Well, there's one happily married couple, anyway.'

> DOROTHY PARKER
> *Too Bad*

Their long years together had shown him that it did not so much matter if marriage was a dull duty, as long as it kept the dignity of a duty: lapsing from that, it became a mere battle of ugly appetites.

> EDITH WHARTON
> *The Age of Innocence*

I am the happiest husband in the world. Caroline is a devoted friend who would sacrifice anything for me – even her cousin Ferdinand if necessary ... The moral of all this, believe me, is that the only happy couples are the foursomes.

> HONORÉ DE BALZAC
> *Philosophie de la Vie conjugale*

The rites of marriage continued and were preserved and that was all that mattered, wasn't it?

> MARGARET FORSTER
> *Marital Rites*

We love each other three months, we squabble three years, we tolerate each other thirty years, and then the children start all over again.

> HIPPOLYTE TAINE
> *Vie et opinions de Thomas Graingorge*, 1867

A marriage where not only esteem, but passion is kept awake, is, I am convinced, the most perfect state of sublunary happiness: but it requires great care to keep this tender plant alive.

> FRANCES BROOKE
> *The History of Emily Montague*, 1769

Theirs was that substantial affection which arises (if any arises at all) when the two who are thrown together begin first by knowing the rougher sides of each other's character, and not the best till further on, the romance growing up in the interstices of a mass of hard prosaic reality ... The feeling proves itself to be the only love which is strong as death – that love which many waters cannot quench, nor the floods drown, beside which the passion usually called by the name is evanescent as steam.

> THOMAS HARDY
> *Far from the Madding Crowd*

'How stupid people are to say that the honeymoon is the best time,' said Natasha. 'On the contrary, now is far better.'

> LEO TOLSTOY
> *War and Peace*

I never thought I coud have been guilty of a deceit to my dear dear angel, which I now find I have, when I told you so long and so often that it was impossible to love you better than I did at that time; but I find by this short (though tedious) absence how much less able I am than ever to live without you (thou joy of my life), therefore I beg, if you love me (which were a sin to doubt), that if you think either business or pleasure will keep you beyond next week, that you would send the coach for me.

> ELIZABETH, LADY BRISTOL
> in a letter to her husband, John Hervey, 28 April 1715
> *The Letter-Books of John Hervey*

She gave me eyes, she gave me ears;
And humble cares, and delicate fears;
A heart, the fountain of sweet tears;
And love, and thought, and joy.

> WILLIAM WORDSWORTH
> 'The Sparrow's Nest', referring to his wife

Yet I *do* not regret that this separation has been, for it is worth so small sacrifice to be thus assured, that instead of weakening, our union has strengthened … Oh William I can not tell thee how I love thee, and thou not desire it – but feel it, O feel it in the fullness of thy soul and *believe* that I am the happiest of Wives & of Mothers & of all Women the most blessed.

> MARY WORDSWORTH
> in a letter to William Wordsworth, 23 May 1812

If ever two were one, then surely we.
If ever man were lov'd by wife, then thee;
If ever wife was happy in a man,
Compare with me ye women if you can.
I prize thy love more than whole Mines of gold,
Or all the riches that the East doth hold.
My love is such that rivers cannot quench,
Nor ought but love from thee, give recompence.
ANN BRADSTREET
17th century

When I reflect tis but 8 daies since we parted, I look back
with wonder; for to me it seems as many years.
ELIZABETH, LADY BRISTOL
in a letter to her husband, John Hervey, 16 August
1721

Ickworth, Wednesday 16 August 1721

past nine at night

My ever-new delight

Was it not enough for my poor soul to bear the pain &
punishment of your absence at so great a distance, but that
I must also endure ye additional affliction of living as many
daies as I have done under the cruel and tedious uncertainty
of your having gott safe and well to Bath; which at this hour
I am still ignorant of, after having expected that releif all
yesterday & thinking my self sure of it to night; but tis now
dark, & no news yet that ye coach is arrived.
JOHN HERVEY, 1st Earl of Bristol
in a letter to his wife Elizabeth
The Letter-Books of John Hervey

That quiet mutual gaze of a trusting husband and wife is like the first moment of rest or refuge from a great weariness or a great danger.
> GEORGE ELIOT
> *Silas Marner*

In the name of my wife I write the completion of hope, and the summit of happiness. To have such a love is the one blessing, in comparison of which all earthly joy is of no value; and to think of her, is to praise God.
> W.M. THACKERAY
> *Henry Esmond*

We've been together now for forty years,
An' it don't seem a day too much;
There ain't a lady livin' in the land
As I'd swop for my dear old Dutch.
> ALBERT CHEVALIER
> popular song, 1900s

Thousands of tedious days and nights are gone
Since thou, my dear, didst leave me here alone,
My days darker than other nights have been,
My nights all black, as black as was ye sin
That caus'd our separation, dearest dust.
Heaven which did joyne us once, that Heaven is just,
And will again unite us in ye grave,
(For I'll no other second marriage have) ...
> SIR THOMAS HERVEY
> on the fourth anniversary of his wife Isabella's death
> in 1686 after 28 years together
> *The Letter-Books of John Hervey*

John Anderson my jo, John,
We clamb the hill thegither;
And mony a jolly day, John,
We've had wi'ane anither:
Now we maun totter down, John,
And hand in hand we'll go;
And sleep thigither at the foot,
John Anderson my jo.
    ROBERT BURNS
    'John Anderson'

Love seems the swiftest, but it is the slowest of all growths.
No man or woman really knows what perfect love is until
they have been married a quarter of a century.
    MARK TWAIN
    Notebook

And such bliss is there between them two
That, save the joy that lasteth evermore,
There is none like, that any creature
Hath seen or shall, while that the world may dure.
    CHAUCER
    'Tale of the Man of Law', *The Canterbury Tales*